Pele

THE FIRE GODDESS

AS TOLD BY DIETRICH VAREZ
AND PUA KANAKA'OLE KANAHELE

ILLUSTRATED BY DIETRICH VAREZ

BISHOP MUSEUM PRESS, 1991

Copyright © 1991 by Bishop Museum
Honolulu, Hawaiʻi
W. Donald Duckworth, Director

Reprinted in 1993

Library of Congress Catalog Card Number 91-072829
ISBN 0-930897-52-8 (hardcover)

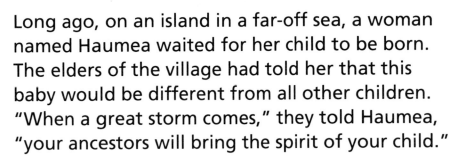

Long ago, on an island in a far-off sea, a woman named Haumea waited for her child to be born. The elders of the village had told her that this baby would be different from all other children. "When a great storm comes," they told Haumea, "your ancestors will bring the spirit of your child."

And so one night, after many months, when the earth shook, lightning split the sky, and thunder rolled down the green valleys, Haumea knew her time had come. She climbed slowly into a large cave above the sea, and here she waited for her child to be born. Outside she could hear the waves pounding on the shore, and the wind blowing black columns of rain through the forest. She felt anxious as the child moved inside her.

When morning came, all was quiet in the cave, except for a small murmur from the bundle wrapped in tapa cloth that Haumea held close to her. Silently, the elders of the village came in to see the child who was the gift of the ancestors.

They named her Pelehonuamea.

Pelehonuamea lived with her mother and father and her many brothers and sisters near the shore of the island where she was born. The other children loved the water, and dove and splashed all day in it, but Pele didn't play with them. While her brothers and sisters rolled in the waves, she would sit on the rocky shore, watching the many kinds of fish that swam in the tidepools.

From the day she was born, Pele was different from all the other children. Her uncle, Lonomakua, was a wise and important man. He was the keeper of the flame. He knew all the secrets of fire, but until now he had had no one to teach them to.

When Pele was a few days old, Lonomakua looked into her eyes and saw the reflection of fire. Then he knew that she was the child to whom he could teach his secrets. He knew that Pele would be the keeper of the fire that burned deep in the earth.

Pele and her older sister, Nāmaka, could not get along. They fought all the time. As they grew up, the rest of the family began to take sides in their arguments, and soon everyone was quarreling.

Nāmaka blamed Pele and her uncle, Lonomakua, for the hot spots that had begun to appear all over the island. Nāmaka said it was because they were building fires in the large caverns under the earth. Finally, she convinced some of the family that unless Pele left the island they would all be burned.

After many arguments, the family agreed that Pele should leave to look for another fire island to live on. But some of her brothers and sisters loved her so much that they decided to go with her. One of her older brothers built a handsome and strong canoe for their journey. They named the canoe Honuaiākea. They gathered all the things they would need for the voyage. At last they loaded them into Honuaiākea and set off. As they sailed away from their home and family, Pele and her brothers and sisters turned for one last look. They were sailing off to an island they had never seen.

But Pele and her brothers and sisters were not afraid of the great ocean. Their family had told them that a guardian spirit, an older brother named Kamohoali'i, would come to them in the form of a shark and would keep them safe.

Before they left, Lonomakua had given Pele a magic stick named Pā'oa. He said it would help her find the fire island that would be her new home.

Pele's mother, Haumea, gave Pele a large egg wrapped in tapa cloth. "Always keep it warm," she told Pele. "This egg will be your companion."

Pele and her brothers and sisters sailed on and on for many months. She thought about her mother, Haumea, making bark cloth, and about her uncle, Lonomakua, in the fire caverns. She longed for them and wondered if she would ever see them again.

One evening Pele called out across the sea to her father, Kānehoalani, and asked him to show her which stars to follow. When a star to the northeast shone brighter than all the others, she knew he had heard her, and they sailed toward it.

The next morning Pele woke early. She smelled something familiar in the air. It was still dark, but far away in the distance she saw a red glow.

The sun rose slowly in the sky. As Pele and her brothers and sisters sailed closer to the glow, their hearts beat anxiously. They could see large mountains. A smoky haze hid their peaks. The familiar scent was the smoke of a volcano erupting. Pele and her brothers and sisters were filled with joy. Pele knew she had found her new home. She called out again to Kānehoalani and thanked her father for bringing them to a fire island. She named it Hawai'i.

Once they had landed on the island, Pele took her magic stick, Pāʻoa, to look for the fire. She found it everywhere. She took Pāʻoa up the mountain until she came to a huge pit, where the top of the volcano had fallen in. Pele spoke to her Gods, and told them that this place was now theirs. She named it Kīlauea. Inside the large pit was a crater, which she named Halemaʻumaʻu. This was her new home where she would live with her brothers and sisters. Pele spoke to her Gods again, telling them that the high cliff to the west of Halemaʻumaʻu would be a sacred place. She named it for the shark-brother who had protected her on her way to the island. That cliff is still known as Ka-pali-kapu-o-Kamohoaliʻi, the sacred cliff of Kamohoaliʻi.

Pele explored her new home. She recognized some plants, but there were others she had never seen before. Her favorite was a small red berry that grew all around her new home. She tasted it, and it was sweet and good. Its pink color reminded her of a friend she had left behind, so she named it for her, Ka'ōhelo. This fruit would always have special meaning for Pele.

Pele soon found a fire God living on Kīlauea. His name was 'Ailā'au, which means forest-eater, and he burned everything he touched. He and Pele both wanted Kīlauea for their home. Pele was determined to keep Kīlauea. She had dedicated the volcano to her Gods, and she could not give it up.

'Ailā'au and Pele started throwing fireballs at each other. Then they began to shake the earth. Then they made the volcano erupt, each one making more flames, smoke, and lava than the other. Lava flowed down Kīlauea to Puna, then to Ka'ū, and finally as far as Kona. The sky was black with smoke.

At last one day the battle ended, and Hawai'i was quiet again. It took a long time for the trade winds to blow the black smoke out to sea. When the air was finally clear, 'Ailā'au was gone. Some people say he hid in the caverns under the earth and may still be wandering down there.

When Pele had beaten 'Ailā'au, the people who lived below Kīlauea respected her as a Goddess. They loved her and were afraid of her too. They brought her gifts and wrote songs for her, and they formed family clans to protect her sacred fire.

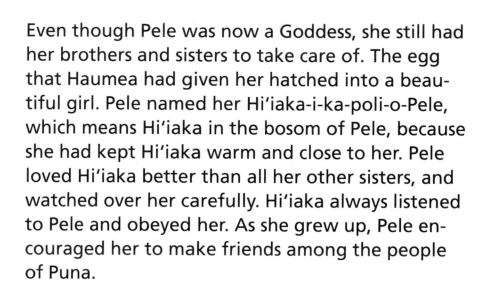

Even though Pele was now a Goddess, she still had her brothers and sisters to take care of. The egg that Haumea had given her hatched into a beautiful girl. Pele named her Hi'iaka-i-ka-poli-o-Pele, which means Hi'iaka in the bosom of Pele, because she had kept Hi'iaka warm and close to her. Pele loved Hi'iaka better than all her other sisters, and watched over her carefully. Hi'iaka always listened to Pele and obeyed her. As she grew up, Pele encouraged her to make friends among the people of Puna.

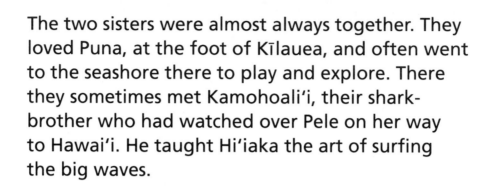

The two sisters were almost always together. They loved Puna, at the foot of Kīlauea, and often went to the seashore there to play and explore. There they sometimes met Kamohoali'i, their shark-brother who had watched over Pele on her way to Hawai'i. He taught Hi'iaka the art of surfing the big waves.

On one of their visits to the seashore, Hiʻiaka made a new friend, a young girl named Hōpoe. She taught Hiʻiaka how to make leis out of the beautiful red *lehua* blossoms, and she danced the hula for her. The two girls became the best of friends.

Pele resented their friendship. She reminded Hiʻiaka that Hōpoe was not a member of the fire clan and warned her that Hōpoe was not the right kind of friend for her.

While Pele wondered how to discourage Hi'iaka's friendship with Hōpoe, she fell asleep under a *hala* tree and had a dream. She dreamed that she was on another island and heard drums beating. As she came closer to the sound, she saw a handsome young man dancing the hula. He danced beautifully, and Pele fell in love with him. He told her that his name was Lohi'au and that he was a chief of the island of Kaua'i.

Pele woke suddenly from her dreams. She decided that Lohi'au must come to live with her.

Pele decided to send Hiʻiaka to Kauaʻi to bring Lohiʻau back to her. She thought this would be a way to discourage Hiʻiaka's friendship with Hōpoe. Hiʻiaka agreed to do what Pele asked. Pele told her younger sister how handsome Lohiʻau was, and warned her not to become too friendly with him. She told Hiʻiaka she must be back with Lohiʻau within forty days, or else she would punish them. Hiʻiaka promised Pele she would do everything she asked.

Pele helped Hi'iaka prepare for the journey to Kaua'i. She gave her a *pā'ū,* a magic skirt that would protect her from danger. As she left, Hi'iaka begged Pele not to hurt her friend Hōpoe. Pele promised, and the two sisters sealed their promises to each other with a kiss.

As Hi'iaka started out, she met a young woman named Wahine'ōma'o. She was carrying a black pig as a gift to Pele. Hi'iaka liked the woman and asked if she would come along on the journey. Wahine'ōma'o said she would, as soon as she had taken the pig offering to Pele. And so they began their adventure.

Hiʻiaka and Wahineʻōmaʻo took a trail that led
through the deep forest of Panaʻewa. In this forest
there lived a large lizard demon, also named
Panaʻewa. He was hard to see among the trees,
because he was covered with scales that looked
like leaves, and his tongue looked like the trunk
of a tree.

Hiʻiaka could feel that Panaʻewa was near even
before she saw him. Quickly and quietly, she got
her *pāʻū* ready. Then Panaʻewa came at them.
Hiʻiaka and the demon lizard fought fiercely, and
when the battle was finally over, Panaʻewa lay
dead, killed by Hiʻiaka and her magical *pāʻū*.

After their battle with Pana'ewa, Hi'iaka and Wahine'ōma'o traveled to Hilo and then went northward to the beautiful green valley of Honoli'i. The beach at the mouth of the valley was a famous surfing spot, and the two girls looked longingly at the waves, but they remembered Pele's orders to hurry back and didn't stop to enjoy the surf.

The stream in Honoli'i was wide and deep, and Hi'iaka knew they couldn't cross it alone. "Hina-hina-ku-i-ka-pali!" she called loudly, and a large and very old turtle crawled out of the stream, looking cross. They climbed on his back, and he slowly paddled them across, grumbling all the way.

The trip to Kaua'i was long and hard, and Hi'iaka and Wahine'ōma'o were tired when they finally reached the island. There they found everyone weeping. When Hi'iaka asked why, they answered, "Lohi'au is dead."

Hi'iaka knew how angry Pele would be if she came back without Lohi'au. She had to act quickly. So she asked to see the place where his body was resting. When she saw Lohi'au lying there, she called on her Gods for help. They answered, and told her what herbs and chants would bring his wandering spirit back to his body. Hi'iaka followed their instructions, and Lohi'au, the young chief of Kaua'i, came back to life.

Hi'iaka explained to Lohi'au why she had come. He was grateful to her for bringing him back to life and curious to meet Pele, so he agreed to return to Puna with her.

By this time almost forty days had passed. Pele had been waiting impatiently, and when there was no sign of Hi'iaka or Lohi'au, she began to suspect they had fallen in love and were never coming back. Jealous and angry, Pele decided to punish Hi'iaka. She started an eruption that flowed toward Hōpoe's home.

Hōpoe saw the fiery river of hot lava moving toward her. Standing at the edge of the ocean, she did the only thing she could think of that might please Pele and change her mood. She danced the hula. She danced beautifully, but nothing stopped the flow of lava.

When at last Hi'iaka arrived in Puna with Lohi'au, she saw a girl made of stone standing at the edge of the sea, and she knew that Pele had broken her promise. Hi'iaka was filled with sadness and anger. She decided to take revenge. Leading Lohi'au to the edge of the crater where Pele could see them, she put her arms around him and embraced him. Furious, Pele covered Lohi'au with lava and flames.

The anger soon went out of the two sisters when they saw what their hot tempers had made them do. Hōpoe and Lohi'au, whom they loved, were both dead. Pele, realizing her shortcomings, promised Hi'iaka she would never doubt her again, and told her she would bring Lohi'au back to life. To show her sister how sorry she was, she said that she would let Lohi'au choose between them. Pele was sure he would choose her.

Pele brought Lohi'au back to life, but he did not choose her. He chose Hi'iaka. Although she was unhappy, Pele kept her promise and gave them her aloha and blessing as they sailed back to Kaua'i.

Pele still lives on Hawai'i, where she rules as the Goddess of volcanoes. The sulphur in the air reminds the people that she is there, alive in her home, Halema'uma'u. Her fiery lava is still pushing eastward toward the rising sun. And year after year, people sing songs and tell stories about Pele of Kīlauea.

E ola mau, e Pele e!
'Eli'eli kau mai!

Long life to you, Pele!

Designed by Barbara Pope